Dropping In On...
Dallas

Judy Greenspan

rourkeeducationalmedia.com

Before Reading:

Building Academic Vocabulary and Background Knowledge

Before reading a book, it is important to tap into what your child or students already know about the topic. This will help them develop their vocabulary, increase their reading comprehension, and make connections across the curriculum.

1. Look at the cover of the book. What will this book be about?
2. What do you already know about the topic?
3. Let's study the Table of Contents. What will you learn about in the book's chapters?
4. What would you like to learn about this topic? Do you think you might learn about it from this book? Why or why not?
5. Use a reading journal to write about your knowledge of this topic. Record what you already know about the topic and what you hope to learn about the topic.
6. Read the book.
7. In your reading journal, record what you learned about the topic and your response to the book.
8. After reading the book complete the activities below.

Content Area Vocabulary
Read the list. What do these words mean?

acrobats
border
centennial
clue
cultures
design
heritage
landmark
modern
pioneer
plains

After Reading:

Comprehension and Extension Activity

After reading the book, work on the following questions with your child or students in order to check their level of reading comprehension and content mastery.

1. How has Dallas changed since it was founded? (Summarize)
2. What makes Dallas an exciting place to live or visit? (Infer)
3. Why might Dallas be considered a sports town? (Asking questions)
4. What interesting things can you find to do and see in Dallas? (Text to self connection)
5. What happened there that changed U.S. history? (Asking questions)

Extension Activity
Draw the outline of a map of Dallas. Inside the city outline, draw the buildings, famous people, and sights that make the city unique.

Table of Contents

Dallas Facts

Founded: 1841
Land area: 340 square miles
(880.59 square kilometers)
Elevation: 450-750 feet
(137-228 meters) above sea level
Previous names: none
Population: 1.25 million
Average Daytime Temperatures:
winter: 58.7 degrees Fahrenheit
(14.7 degrees Celsius)
spring: 76.7 degrees Fahrenheit
(24.7 degrees Celsius)
summer: 94.7 degrees Fahrenheit
(35 degrees Celsius)
fall: 78.3 degrees Fahrenheit
(26 degrees Celsius)

Ethnic diversity:
White 28.8%%
Hispanic or Latino 42.4%
African-American 25%
Asian 2.9%
American Indian or Alaska Native .7%

City Nicknames:
Big D

Number of Visitors Annually:
22.6 million

The "Big D"

Are you ready to meet a giant cowboy named Big Tex? Eat a fried peanut butter banana cheeseburger? Journey into space and travel back in time? Then let's go! We're dropping in on Dallas, Texas. The "Big D" is a big city in a big state with a lot to see and do.

Look at Texas on the map. It's hard to miss. Texas is the second biggest state in the United States. Only Alaska is bigger.

Dallas is in North Texas, right next to the Trinity River, the longest river in the state. Trinity means "a group of three." Dallas was settled where three branches of the river joined into one.

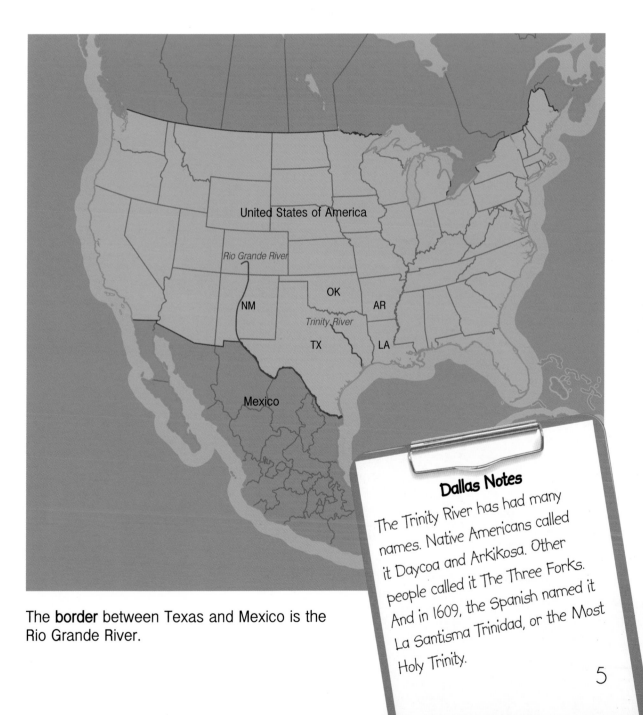

The **border** between Texas and Mexico is the Rio Grande River.

Dallas Notes

The Trinity River has had many names. Native Americans called it Daycoa and Arkikosa. Other people called it The Three Forks. And in 1609, the Spanish named it La Santisma Trinidad, or the Most Holy Trinity.

Flying over Dallas today, you see a big city with tall buildings surrounded by flat land. That's because Dallas is on the edge of the Great **Plains**. The Great Plains are about 2,500 miles (4,023 kilometers) long and stretch all the way from Texas to Canada.

Dallas

Great Plains

In Dallas, there are great buildings, too: old and new, different kinds and lots of shapes. See that one with the ball on the top? Hundreds of feet high, it's called Reunion Tower and it's a Dallas **landmark**. A glass elevator zooms to the top in just 68 seconds. That's much faster than climbing up the tower's 837 steps.

A landmark is something people recognize. It can be a building, a mountain, or even a flying red horse. In Dallas, Pegasus, the flying red horse, is one of the city's most famous landmarks.

From the top of Reunion Tower, you can see the entire city of Dallas.

The original Pegasus was on top of Dallas's Magnolia Hotel. A new Pegasus is perched there today.

7

Looking down from Reunion Tower, you can see another Dallas landmark. This old red building is often called Old Red. It looks like a red brick castle, but it was a courthouse when it opened back in 1892.

THE OLD RED MUSEUM, INSIDE OLD RED, IS A GREAT PLACE TO LEARN ABOUT THE HISTORY OF DALLAS.

Not far from Old Red, you'll find Fountain Place Plaza. There are 26,000 windows on this shiny skyscraper, which rises high above a plaza filled with bubbling water fountains.

How about one more landmark? This is Dallas City Hall. It doesn't look like the other buildings. But it does look like it might tip over!

This is Dallas's fifth city hall building. It opened in 1978.

There are lots of buildings, and lots of people in Dallas, too. In fact, Dallas is the third biggest city in the state of Texas. More than 1,200,000 people call it home.

But life was much different in Dallas back in 1841.

The merengue is sometimes called the national dance of the Dominican Republic.

History Mystery

What's a log cabin doing in the middle of Dallas? Looks pretty strange, doesn't it? But this log cabin is a **clue** to the past. In 1841, a **pioneer** named John Neely Bryan (1810–1877) lived along the Trinity River. He built a log cabin like this one, then began to build a town. That town would become the city of Dallas.

John said he named the town "after my friend, Dallas." But who was his friend Dallas? Was it George Mifflin Dallas, the Vice President of the United States? Or George's brother, Alexander Dallas? Or maybe a brave soldier named Walter Dallas? Turns out, no one really knows.

This log cabin is a replica, or copy, of John Neely Bryan's cabin.

We do know, however, that by 1850, 430 people lived in Dallas. And ten years later, there were 3,000. Cotton was a growing business and when the railroad came to town, business started booming.

A HUGE CROWD GATHERED TO CELEBRATE THE NEW RAILROAD IN 1872 WITH A BUFFALO BARBECUE.

BACK THEN, PEOPLE CALLED THE NEW TRAINS, "IRON HORSES." CAN YOU GUESS WHY?

Visitors are allowed to feed the giraffes fresh green lettuce at the Dallas Zoo.

Dallas Notes

As the city grew, so did the Dallas Zoo. There were just four animals when the zoo opened in 1888: two mountain lions and two deer. Now the Dallas Zoo has thousands of animals including gorillas, chimpanzees, giraffes, elephants, and anteaters.

13

What was it like to live in Dallas long ago? You can find out at the Dallas **Heritage** Village. There are 38 old buildings here, all built between 1840 and 1910. You can go into an old train station, a doctor's office, or a school house. Have a root beer float in an old-time saloon. Or go to work in the General Store and ring up a sale on an old-fashioned cash register.

The old buildings in the Dallas Heritage Village were originally from many different places in Texas.

Dallas Notes
The Dallas Public Library owns an original copy of the United States Declaration of Independence.

14

There are lots of ways to visit the past in Dallas. The Dallas Firefighters Museum is inside a real fire station built in 1907. Compare the fire engines you see here to **modern** fire engines. Can you imagine horses pulling this steam pump as they raced to a fire?

Firefighters no longer used steam pumps by the early part of the 1900s.

Speaking of horses, these cowboys look so real you can almost hear them yelling "Giddy-up!" The statues in Pioneer Plaza Cattle Drive are quite a sight! Three huge bronze cowboys rounding up 49 enormous bronze cattle remind us of real cattle drives from long ago.

There are no cattle drives in downtown Dallas these days, but you can see real cowboys every summer at the Mesquite Championship Rodeo. They do everything from bareback riding to bull riding to barrel racing.

Cowgirls and cowboys like this one compete over the course of 12 weeks for a spot in the Mesquite Championship Rodeo finals.

Sweat Beads and Shadetrees

If you're wondering how high the temperature rises in Dallas, well, that depends on the season. Fall slowly cools down and winter sometimes gets cold. Spring is often stormy and summer is always hot, often more than 100 degrees Fahrenheit (37.78 degrees Celsius). These days, most people turn on the air conditioner. But long ago, it was hard to beat the summer heat.

People in Dallas used to put buckets of ice in front of electric fans to try to cool the air. There were special words to describe the heat:

Sweat beads: Drops of sweat that looked like a necklace around someone's neck.

Shadetree: Trees for shading people.

April showers may bring May flowers, but Dallas starts blooming in February. At the Dallas Arboretum and Botanical Garden, you can see thousands of flowers, including tulips, daffodils, pansies, and blue bonnets, the Texas State flower.

There's a flower festival at the Arboretum every spring called Dallas Blooms.

Cool Culture

Luckily, there are plenty of cool places to go when the Dallas sun blazes.

At the Dallas World Aquarium, there are giant river otters, sea turtles, catfish, penguins, and other creatures from around the world.

At the Perot Museum of Nature and Science, you can take a video journey into space, zoom to the moon, and then drop by Mercury and Venus. You can experiment with fruit flies and **design** your own robot, too.

Things can get wild at the Dallas World Aquarium! Sloths like this one live there along with the aquatic creatures.

Speaking of robots, you can find three robot-like sculptures called the Traveling Man in Dallas's Deep Ellum neighborhood. Originally known as a "freedmen's town," Deep Ellum was settled by freed slaves after the Civil War.

By the 1920s, Deep Ellum was a famous place to hear the best blues and jazz musicians.

Dallas Notes
The main road in Deep Ellum is Elm Street. Locals used to say Ellum instead of Elm. That's how Deep Ellum got its name.

No visit to Dallas is complete without a trip to Fair Park. Built in 1936 to celebrate the Texas State **Centennial**–Texas's 100th birthday–the park spreads across hundreds of acres and includes gardens, museums, a children's aquarium, a band shell, a music hall, and the famous Cotton Bowl sports stadium.

There are 92,100 seats in the Cotton Bowl Stadium.

Dressed in colorful costumes, flamenco dancers are fun to watch at the State Fair.

Every fall, Fair Park is home to the Texas State Fair. It began in 1886 and is now the biggest state fair in the United States. For almost a month, there are pig races, dog shows, tractor pulls, food stands, horses, cows, **acrobats**, and concerts.

What makes those pigs run? A delicious chocolate prize at the finish line.

And towering over it all? The biggest cowboy in Texas, Big Tex himself. All 55 feet (16.76 meters) of him.

This is the second Big Tex at the Texas State Fair. The first Big Tex was ruined in a fire in 2012.

Big Tex's Measurements

1. His hands: Five feet six inches long (l.7 meters)
2. His head: Ten feet high (3.1 meters)
3. His boots: 12 feet long (3.66 meters)
4. His waist: 27 feet around (8.23 meters)
5. His shirt sleeves: 27 feet long (8.23 meters)
6. His weight: 25,000 pounds (11,340 kilograms)

A Fried What?

There's plenty of food at the State Fair and it's a Texas tradition to serve it up fried. Every year, there are new favorites to choose from. Here are a few you can try:

- Fried bubble gum
- Fried peanut butter and jelly sandwiches
- Fried pumpkin pie
- Fried peanut butter banana cheeseburgers
- Deep fried milk and cookies on a stick

Deep fried Coca Cola includes whipped cream and a cherry.

The Texas Star Ferris wheel is even taller than Big Tex, rising 212 feet (64.6 meters) in the air.

What's Big in Dallas?

It's no surprise that with a nickname like the "Big D," Dallas is known for big things.

Big sports teams: the Cowboys (National Football League), Rangers (Major League Baseball), Mavericks (National Basketball Association), and Stars (National Hockey League).

Big ideas: Barney the purple dinosaur was invented here. So were snow cones, corn dogs, Doritos, laser tag, microchips, and handheld calculators.

Big History: In 1908, there was a big flood when the Trinity River overflowed.

In 1930, C.M. "Dad" Joiner struck big oil just east of Dallas.

And on November 22, 1963 at 12:30 p.m., John F. Kennedy, the 35th President of the United States, was shot and killed in Dallas. Today, not far from John Neely Bryan's cabin, the Sixth Floor Museum tells the sad story of what happened that day and how it changed Dallas, the country, and the world.

The Sixth Floor Museum is in a building once called the Texas School Book Depository.

It's hard to believe that Dallas was once a tiny town with dirt roads and log cabins. Look how pretty the city is at night! Pegasus the flying red horse shines brightly in the sky and the great buildings of all shapes and sizes glow with colorful lights.

If he could see it today, what do you think John Neely Bryan would say about the city he started?

Timeline

1841
John Neely Bryan settles along the Trinity River.

1845
The United States annexes Texas. Texas becomes the country's 28th state.

1846
Dallas County is founded.

1865
Freed slaves build "Freedman's Towns" around the city. The most famous is called Deep Ellum.

1872-1873
Arrival of the first and second railroads in Dallas.

1882
Opening season for the Dallas Hams, the city's first baseball team.

1886
The first Texas State Fair is held.

1888
The Dallas Zoo Opens.

1891
Dallas Football Club is formed.

1892
Old Red Courthouse is built.

1901
The first Dallas Public Library opens.

1907
Dallas becomes one of the largest cotton markets.

1908
The Trinity River floods.

1919
The first snow cones are sold at the Texas State Fair.

1930
C.M. "Dad" Joiner strikes oil.

1936
Texas Centennial opens in Fair Park.

1960
National Football League's Dallas Cowboys are founded.

1963
President Kennedy is shot.

1967
Handheld calculators are invented.

1974
Dallas Fort Worth Airport opens.

1995
Ron Kirk becomes the first African-American mayor.

Glossary

acrobats (AK-ruh-bats): people who perform exciting gymnastics acts that require great skill

border (BOR-dur): the dividing line between two places

centennial (sen-ten-ee-uhl): the 100th year celebration of an event

clue (kloo): an object or piece of information that helps you answer a question or solve a mystery

cultures (kuhl-churs): the ideas, customs, traditions, and ways of life of groups of people

design (di-zine): to draw a plan for something that can be made

heritage (HER-i-tij): traditions and beliefs that a country or society considers an important part of its history

landmark (LAND-mahrk): an object in a landscape that stands out

modern (MAH-durn): having to do with the present or recent times

pioneer (pye-uh-neer): a person who explores new territory and settles there

plains (playns): large, flat areas of land

Index

Show What You Know

1. Why is there an old log cabin in the middle of Dallas?
2. When was Fair Park opened and what was Texas celebrating?
3. How much does Big Tex weigh?
4. Dallas is near the Trinity River. Why do you think so many cities are built along rivers?
5. Who was Dallas named after?

Websites to Visit

https://tpwd.texas.gov/kids/
www.visittheusa.com/usa/states/texas/cities/dallas.aspx
www.watermelon-kid.com/history/dallas/

About the Author

Judy Greenspan grew up near Boston and always enjoyed exploring the city. She especially liked finding good stories about the past. Today, Judy works in a New York City museum and creates programs about city life a century ago. She was also a television producer for many years and now lives in Manhattan with her husband and two daughters.

Meet The Author!
www.meetREMauthors.com

© 2016 Rourke Educational Media

www.rourkeeducationalmedia.com

PHOTO CREDITS: Cover © Andreykrav, Weling01, David Sucsy; Title Page, Page 7: © Davel15957; Page 4: © Paul Komarek, antoniodiaz; Page 6: © franckreporter; Page 7: © Dorti; Page 8: © dnaveh; Page 9: © Aneese, wellesenterprises; Page 10: © Lord-Kuernyus; Page 11, 29: © Library of Congress; Page 12: © csp7596761; Page 13, 29: © Kevin1086, Vlad-Pod; Page 14: © Prisma Bildagentur, AG/Alamy Stock Photo; Page 15: © MCCAIG; Page 16: © Camerashots; Page 17: © Scott Goodno/Alamy Stock Photo; Page 18: © Lopolo; Page 19: © Howard Sach; Page 20: © Sergiodelgado; Page 21: © wenling01; Page 23: © LS Photos/Alamy Stock Photo, inababes; Page 24: © Anthony Aneese Totah Jr.; Page 25: © David R. Tribble, National Geographic Image Collection/Alamy Stock Photos; Page 26: © Ken Durden, Jordan Shaw, nicescene; Page 27: © Daryl Lang; Page 28: © Andreykrav, Dorti; Page 29: © Ken Durden, Kevin1086, David R. Tribble

Edited by: Keli Sipperley

Illustrations by: Caroline Romanet

Cover and interior design by: Jen Thomas

Library of Congress PCN Data

Dropping in on Dallas / Judy Greenspan
ISBN 978-1-68191-407-7 (hard cover)
ISBN 978-1-68191-449-7 (soft cover)
ISBN 978-1-68191-487-9 (e-Book)
Library of Congress Control Number: 2015951573

Printed in the United States of America, North Mankato, Minnesota

Also Available as:

ROURKE'S
e-Books